SKETCHES
OF THE
MYTHOLOGY
AND
CUSTOMS
OF THE
HINDOOS

SKETCHES

OF THE

MYTHOLOGY

AND

CUSTOMS

OF THE

HINDOOS

MOST RESPECTFULLY INSCRIBED

TO THE HONORABLE THE

COURT OF DIRECTORS

OF THE

EAST-INDIA COMPANY

GEORGE FORSTER

GYAN

Published by

Gyan Publishing House
5, Ansari Road
Daryaganj, New Delhi-110002
Phone: 011-47034999, 9811692060
E-mail: books@gyanbooks.com

Distribution Network
gyanbooks.com
India, USA, Canada, UK, Australia

ISBN: 978-93-6780-744-6 (PB)

First Published, 1785

2nd Impression 2024

Printed at: Gyan Press, Delhi.

SKETCHES OF THE MYTHOLOGY AND CUSTOMS OF THE HINDOOS
Author: GEORGE FORSTER

SKETCHES

OF THE

MYTHOLOGY

AND

CUSTOMS

OF THE

HINDOOS.

LONDON:

PRINTED IN THE YEAR

MDCCLXXXV.

SKETCHES

OF THE

MYTHOLOGY

AND

CUSTOMS

OF THE

HINDOOS,

MOST RESPECTFULLY INSCRIBED

TO THE HONORABLE THE

COURT OF DIRECTORS

OF THE

EAST-INDIA COMPANY,

BY THEIR DUTIFUL SERVANT,

GEORGE FORSTER.

London,
July, 1785.

THE following cursory dissertation, which has been extracted from private letters, the Author is induced to lay before the Public, from a desire of throwing some light on a subject, hitherto, but partially known in Europe; and also, with the view of prompting others, whose bent of disposition and conveniency of situation may lead them into such researches, to enlarge on so curious a matter.

To hold out an asylum to the memory of an antient, and a once great people, who before the fall of *of their empire were amply enlightened by ſcience, and who were governed by a ſyſtem of laws and policy, which had the most ſalutary effects in rendering them virtuous and happy, will yield a ſufficient compenſation to the man of philanthropy, for every difficulty that he may encounter in the purſuit of a ſtudy which will be found, it is to be feared, entangled in ſome diſcouraging perplexities.*

Extract of a Letter, dated at Banaris in September, 1782.

THE city of Banaris, in point of its wealth, coſtly buildings, and the number of its inhabitants, is claſſed in the firſt rank of thoſe now remaining in Hinduſtan, in the poſ-ſeſſion of the Hindoos.

To deſcribe, with any degree of preciſion, the various temples dedi-cated in this place to the almoſt innumerable deities, and to explain the origin of their foundation, with the neceſſary arrangement, would require a knowledge, infinitely ſuperior to mine, in the myſterious rites of the Hindoo mythology.

They are, at this day, enveloped in ſuch impenetrable obſcurity, that even thoſe Pundits who are the moſt ſkilfully verſed in the Sumſcrit,* are not able to throw on them lights ſufficiently clear for the rendering them comprehenſible to the generality of the people.

But as ſome relation, though imperfect, of a city ſo famous in Hinduſtan, and now ſo well known in

* The language in which all their ſacred legends are preſerved.

Europe

Europe for having been one of the grand ſources of the religious worſhip of the Hindoos, and being the chief repoſitory of what ſcience yet exiſts among them, may not be unacceptable to you, together with ſome curſory inveſtigations of the mythology of Brimha, the taſk ſhall be attempted with every attention to the ſubject, and with the ſtricteſt adherence to truth.

If errors ſhould ariſe on the treating on a matter hitherto ſlightly diſcuſſed, and from its complication exceedingly abſtruſe, I have to intreat your liberal indulgence; and that though miſtaken in my concluſions, you will give me ſome commendation were it only for the endeavour of adminiſtering to a rational pleaſure.

At the diſtance of eight miles from the city of Banaris, as it is approached on the river from the eaſtward, the eye is attracted by the view of two lofty minarets, which were erected by the order of Aurungzebe, on the foundation of an ancient Hindoo temple, dedicated to the Mhah Deve, or the God Eiſhwer.

The raiſing, on ſuch ſacred ruins, this towering Mahometan pile, which from its elevated height ſeems to look down with triumph and exaltation on the fallen ſtate of a city ſo profoundly revered by the Hindoos, would appear to have been prompted to the mind of Aurungzebe by a bigotted and intemperate deſire of inſulting their religion.

If ſuch was his wiſh, it hath been moſt completely fulfilled.

For the Hindoos conſider this monument as a diſgraceful record of a foreign yoke, and as proclaiming to every ſtranger, that their favorite city has been debaſed, and the worſhip of their gods defiled.

From the top of the minarets there is ſeen an entire and a very beautiful proſpect of Banaris, which occupies a ſpace of about two miles and a half along the northern bank of the Ganges, and a mile inland from the river.

Many of the houſes are remarkably high, ſome of them having ſix and ſeven ſtories, and built of a ſtone reſembling that ſort found in the quarries

ries of Portland, and which abounds in this part of the country.

The ſtreets, wherein theſe lofty buildings are ſituated, are ſo narrow as not to admit of two carriages abreaſt.

The conſequence of this large city being conſtructed on ſo confined a plan, is, that the air, from being deprived of a free circulation, becomes putrid and obnoxious, and in particular ſeaſons cauſes fevers of a malignant ſpecies, and ſevere bilious obſtructions.

In addition to this pernicious effect, proceeding from a corrupted atmoſphere, there is at moſt times an intolerable ſtench, which ariſes from the many tanks diſperſed in the different

ferent quarters of the town, whoſe waters and borders are appropriated to the common uſe of the inhabitants.

The filth alſo, which is indiſcriminately thrown into the ſtreets, and there left expoſed, (for the Hindoos poſſeſs but a ſmall portion of a general cleanlineſs) add to the compound of ill ſmells which ſo much offend the noſtrils of every one entering this city.

The irregular and very confined mode which has been invariably adhered to in the conſtruction of Banaris, has, in a great meaſure, deſtroyed the pleaſing effects which ſymmetry and arrangement would otherwiſe have beſtowed on a city, entitled from its numerous and expenſive habitations, to demand a preference to any capital which I have ſeen in India.

In the reſearches which I have been enabled to make into the principles of the Hindoo religion, I have received great aid from a converſant knowledge of the Mhahrattah language, and an acquaintance, though trivial, with the Sumſcrit.

The uſe of this laſt tongue is now chiefly confined to a particular ſect of Bramins, who officiate in the character of prieſts, and it hath ever been adopted as the channel of conveying to the Hindoos, the eſſentials of their religion, with all the various forms of their worſhip.

The Sumſcrit is a ſonorous language, its periods flow with great

boldneſs,

boldneſs, and terminate in a cadence peculiarly muſical, and it abounds in a pith and conciſeneſs far ſuperior to any other, with which I am in any wiſe acquainted.

An extract of a ſloke or ſtanza, which has been quoted by Mr. Halhed, is a ſtriking teſtimony of the nervous compoſition, and the laconic turn of the Sumſcrit.

As it is a ſtanza of only four lines, I will inſert it, and alſo attempt the tranſlation.

Pētăche rĕnĕwān ſhĕtrōō
Father — in debt — enemy
Mātāh ſhĕtrōō rĕſhĕlēnēē
Mother — enemy — extravagant or immoral
Bhārĭāh rŭpĕwūttēē ſhĕtrōō
Wife — beautiful — enemy
Pōōtrĕ ſhĕtrōō n'pūndĭtāh
Son — enemy — unlearned

The mother who hath loſt her fame,
The ſire profuſe, and foe to ſhame,
Are to their race a peſt.
A bride's ſoft joys oft' thorns implant,
And he, who roams in folly's haunt,
Deſtroys his father's reſt.

The Hindoos believe in one God, without beginning and without end; on whom they beſtow, deſcriptive of his power, a variety of epithets.

But the moſt common appellation, and which conveys the ſublimeſt ſenſe of his greatneſs, is, Sree Mun Narrain, the univerſal Protector.

The Hindoos, in their firſt and grand ſupplication to the Deity, addreſs him as endowed with the three attri-

attributes, of omnipotence, omnipreſence and omniſcience; which, in the Sumſcrit, are expreſſed by the terms, neer anjin, neer akar, and neer goon.

Though this explanation may not, in literary ſtrictneſs, compriſe in it the preciſe meaning of the Engliſh text, it doth ſo virtually, and in the ampleſt ſenſe.

A circumſtance which forcibly ſtruck my attention, was the Hindoo belief of a Trinity.

The perſons are, Sree Mun Narrain, the Mhah Letchimy (a beautiful woman), and a Serpent, which are emblematical of ſtrength, love and wiſdom.

Theſe perſons, by the Hindoos, are ſuppoſed to be wholly indiviſible.

The one is three, and the three are one.

In the beginning they ſay, that the Deity created three men, to whom he gave the names of Brimha, Vyſtnou, and Shevah.*

To the firſt, was committed the power of creating mankind, to the ſecond of cheriſhing them, and to the third that of reſtraining and correcting them.

Brimha, at one breath, formed the human kind out of the four elements; amongſt which he infuſed, as I underſtood the intrepretation, a vacuum.

* Often called Eiſhwer, or the Mhah Deve.

Before

Before the creation of man, Sree Mun Narrain framed the world out of a chaos; it was covered with the waters, ſurrounded by an utter darkneſs, and inhabited by a demon, the ſuppoſed author of evil, whom the Godhead drove into an abyſs under the earth.

The Hindoos, as Mr. Halhed, in his Tranſlation of the Code of Hindoo Laws, has fully and clearly ſet forth, are arranged in four grand caſts or tribes*; that of the Bramin, the Chittery, the Bhyſe and the Sooder.

* There is, in India, an aboriginal race of people who are not claſſed in any of the ſects, and are employed in the meaneſt and moſt menial offices. They are not permitted to enter any temple of the Hindoos, and in their diet they have no reſtriction. On ſome parts of the coaſt of Choromandel they are called Pariahs, and, in Bengal, Hurrees.

Each

Each of theſe caſts are ſub-divided into numerous ſects, the particular uſages of which are preſerved with great care and attentive diſtinctions.

There is an immenſe number of ſectaries of the ſame tribe, who do not admit of the intercourſe of marriage with each other, or of eating at the ſame board.

From the beſt information which I have been enabled to procure, it would ſeem that the genuine Chittery, or Rajah race, has for a great length of time been extinct, and in its place a ſpurious tribe has been introduced.

The Hindoos, compoſing theſe caſts and claſſes, are ultimately branched out in two diviſions; the one denominated

minated the Vyſtnou Bukht, and the other the Shevah Bukht.

The followers of the firſt are diſtinguiſhed by marking the forehead with a longitudinal, and thoſe of the ſecond with a parallel line.

In the temple of Vyſtnou, he is worſhipped under the repreſentation of a human figure, having a circle of heads and four hands, emblems of an all-ſeeing, and an all-provident Being.

The repreſentation of a fabulous bird, on which he is ſuppoſed to ride, and denotive of the velocity of his motion, is frequently placed in front of his image.

Shevah or Eiſhwer, or as he is uſually called by the Hindoos, the

Mhah Deve, or great God, is repre-ſented by a compound figure, deſ-cribing the male and female parts of generation, and deſigned as ſymbols of procreation and fecundity.

Theſe faculties or qualities being held amongſt the Hindoos as the choiceſt bleſſings, and the deprivation of them deemed a ſevere reproach and misfortune.

Facing this deſignation of the Mhah Deve, is generally ſeen, in a ſuppliant poſture, the image of a cow, which is ſaid to have derived its peculiarly ſacred qualities from having been choſen by this god as his favorite conveyance.

The more enlightened Pundits tell you, that this animal hath been pre-ſerved from ſlaughter from its great utiiity utility to man; it being his ableſt aſ-ſiſtant in the labors of the field, and the chief ſupport in his immediate maintenance.

Not to ſay that it argues a ſound policy to ſtamp this creature with ſo ſacred a mark; for were its fleſh eaten, as Hinduſtan is productive of but few horſes, the various branches of agri-culture would ſuffer an eſſential in-jury.

Another figure repreſents Shevah with four hands (holding in them dif-ferent emblems of his power) and five heads; four of which are directed to the cardinal points, and the fifth is placed with the face upwards, in the act of contemplating the grand Deity.

After the ſervice which Brimhah has performed on earth, it would reaſonably be concluded, that his praiſe for the obligations which mankind have received at his hands, in ſome degree, would be conformable to his works.

But the Hindoos have not dedicated one temple to his honor, nor have they ſet apart or ſanctified one day in remembrance of his deeds.

It would redound but little to my credit, were I to inſert in this place, the reaſon alledged in their religious tracts, for this ſeeming neglect of Brimhah.

It is a tale framed to amuſe the credulous Hindoo, and procure a meal to an artful prieſt.

This

This oſtenſible want of attention to the memory of Brimhah, may on a more abſtracted ground be attributed to the opinion, that the powers of procreation having been once ſet in action, and operating by a law, general and undeviating, whoſe immediate benefits exiſt and are evidently diſplayed in its effects, there was no neceſſity of commemorating the firſt individual cauſe.

The Hindoos believe implicitly in predeſtination, and in the tranſmigration of the ſoul.

The firſt, as it frequently cramps the genius and obſtructs its progreſſion, yet has a tendency in conſoling them in every misfortune, and adminiſtering to them a comfort in all the untoward events of life.

They ſay it is the hand of God, which for ſome inſcrutinable purpoſe directs and impels the actions of his creature.

The doctrine of the metempſychoſis reſtrains them from the uſe of animal food* ; an aliment not neceſſary, and often attended with pernicious conſequences in a hot climate.

This belief has alſo a ſtrong tendency to infuſe into their minds an abhorrence of all ſanguinary acts, and to inculcate the virtues of humanity and a general affection.

* This tenet is not at this day ſtrictly adhered to, for the Hindoos of the ſecond and fourth caſt occaſionally uſe fleſh meats, and the Bramins of Bengal invariably eat fiſh.

The

The Hindoos compute their grand evolutions of time by Joques, of which they have four, correſponding in their nature with the golden, ſilver, brazen, and iron ages of the antients.

The preſent, they ſay, is the Khullee, or the fourth Joque; and that at the expiration of every age, the Supreme Being has deſtroyed this globe of earth, which has been re-created at the commencement of the one ſucceeding, and that a continued ſucceſſion of Joques will revolve *ad infinitum*.

The records of this ancient and extraordinary people, unfortunately for the learned of the preſent day, teem ſo profuſely with fable, and abound throughout in ſuch extravagant relations

tions of the actions of their demi-gods, greatly ſimilar in their feats to the Bacchus, Hercules, and Theſeus of the Greeks, that no rational or ſatisfactory concluſion can be drawn for any adjuſtment of chronology.

A Pundit will introduce into his legend a laack* of years with as much facility, and perhaps conviction to himſelf, as a modern commentator would reduce to his ſtandard half a century.

The principles of the Hindoo religion, with its moſt eſſential tenets, were compoſed, it is aſſerted, by Brimhah, and comprized in four books, entitled the Baids or Vaids, a word

* An hundred thouſand.

ſignifying

ſignifying myſtery in the Sumſcrit language.

In that part of the peninſula of India bordering on the Choromandel ſide, theſe ſacred writings are named the Vaidums.

The Telingahs and the Malabars commonly change the letter B into a V, and invariably terminate all Sumſcrit words with an M.

The Shaſtre, meaning ſcience, is a moſt voluminous commentary on the Baids; and has been written by various Pundits, for the purpoſe of illuſtrating their mythology. From the Shaſtre proceed thoſe prepoſterous and irreconcileably ſuperſtitious ceremonies which have been dragged by their doctors

doctors into the Hindoo ſyſtem of worſhip; all of them tending to ſhackle the vulgar mind, and produce in it a ſlaviſh reverence for the tribe of Bramins.

The privilege of reading the Baids and expounding its texts is only allowed to them, and prohibited under ſevere penalties from the inſpection of the other caſts.

By the ſole inveſtment of this ſingular authority, the prieſt is left at liberty to explain the original doctrine as may be the moſt conducive in conſolidating the power and promoting the intereſts of his order.

In the tranſmigration of the ſoul into different bodies, conſiſts the various gradations of reward and punishment amongst the Hindoos.

Conformably to their good or evil actions they are transposed into the bodies of such creatures, whether of the human or brute species, as by their conduct, whilst in the occupation of their former tenements, they may have merited.

They do not admit of the infliction of eternal punishment, and shudder at the idea of a belief so disconsonant to the opinion which they have formed of the Supreme Being.

Evil dispositions, they say, are chastised by a confinement in the bodies of those animals whose natures they most resemble, and are constrained to occupy them until their vices are either eradicated, or ſo purged as that they ſhall be judged worthy of poſſeſſing ſuperior forms.

The good actions of man, the Hindoo law-giver has written, will be rewarded by their being made to perſonify ſuch beings as enjoy the utmoſt human happineſs.

As that which the magiſtrate experiences on the juſt and merciful execution of the truſt which has been committed to him; or, that high ſenſe of pleaſure which the man of humanity partakes of, when he has alleviated the diſtreſſes of the unfortunate, or otherwiſe promoted the welfare of mankind.

The man who is acceptable in the ſight of his God, the Hindoo ſays, will

will copiously imbibe all those heart-felt satisfactions, which are produced from the well performance of the different duties of life.

After having occupied a series of bodies to the approbation of the Deity and his soul, from a pursuit of virtue, shall be purified from the taints of evil, the Hindoo is then admitted to participation of the radiant and never ceasing glory of his first cause.

The soul's receiving this act of bliss, is described, by comparing it to a ray of light, attracted by the grand powers of the sun, to which it shoots with an immense velocity, and is there absorbed in the blaze of splendor.

Yum Durm Rajah officiates in the same capacity amongst the Hindoos, as Minos did in the infernal regions of the antients.

At the tribunal of Yum Durm, all departed ſouls are ſuppoſed to appear, and their actions are proclaimed aloud by this judge, who paſſes an immediate ſentence.

Should the diſpoſition of a man have been ſo flagitiouſly wicked and depraved, as to be judged unworthy even of an introduction into the body of the vileſt animal, ſuch corporeal torments are impoſed on him as may be thought adequate to the tranſgreſſion, and the ſoul is afterwards placed in ſome ſuitable ſtation on earth.

According to the religious traditions of the Hindoos, Sree Mun Narrain, ſince the creation of the world, has at nine

nine different periods aſſumed incarnated forms for the purpoſe of eradicating ſome particular evil, or otherwiſe chaſtiſing the ſins of mankind.

The Hindoos worſhip a ſecondary ſpecies of deity, which they wildly reckon at the number of the thirty-three krore*, and who in their different functions are deſigned to repreſent the multiplied infinitude of power of the Supreme Deity.

From the croud of images which the Bramin has placed in the temples of the Hindoos, they have been branded with the appellation of idolaters, or adorers of many gods.

Let this mode of offering up ſupplications

* A krore is a hundred laacks.

plications or thankſgivings to the Supreme Being be diſpaſſionately examined, and it may be ſeen, that a perſonification of the attributes of the Deity, is not unfitly adapted to the general comprehenſion.

For thoſe, and they compoſe a great portion of the people, who, from a want of the requiſite education, are not endowed with the ability of reading the praiſe of God, can with facility conceive an idea of his greatneſs, by contemplating a figure, ſculptured with many heads and with many hands, adorned with every ſymbol of human power, and beheld by all claſſes of men with the utmoſt reverence and awe.

Were the origin of emblematical figures deduced with a poſitive degree of of certainty, there would remain little doubt of diſcovering, that they far preceded the uſe of letters.

The Spaniſh records mention, that the intelligence of the firſt arrival of the Europeans on the coaſt of Mexico, was deſcribed to Motezuma by figures painted on cotton cloth.

In a rude ſociety, it was evidently a more eaſy operation to convey an idea thro' the medium of a ſimple figure cut in wood or moulded in clay, than to invent an alphabet, and out of it compoſe an aſſemblage of words neceſſary for the formation of a language.

The immenſe group of Hindoo gods enjoy immortality, which they are gifted with from drinking a beverage, called

called Amrut, and which ſeems to bear ſome analogy to the nectar of Homer's deities.

In their mythology, there is an elegant deſcription of nine goddeſſes, reſembling in a great degree the muſes of the antients, in the nature of their provinces.

There is alſo, moſt pictureſquely delineated, the God of Love, who has a variety of epithets, all ſignificant of the unbounded ſway, which he poſſeſſes over the hearts of men.

His common names are Kaum and Mudden, and he is repreſented as a pleaſing youth, armed with a bow and five arrows, denoting the five ſenſes, each of which weapon is baited with different qualities of the poiſon, which is infused by the communication of the passion of love.

A curious picture was found at Tanjore, when the fort was captured, of Kaum riding on an elephant, whose form was composed of the figures of seven young women, which were entwined together in so ingenious and whimsical a manner, that they exhibited an exact shape of that bulky animal.

In the Biss Eishwer Pagoda at Banaris, there is a design well executed in stone of the God of the Sun, sitting in a chariot and driving a horse with twelve heads, allusive of the twelve signs of the Zodiac.

If the perusal of this rough and abbreviated sketch, should lead on any gentleman eſtabliſhed in this part of the country, and poſſeſſing an inclination to this caſt of inveſtigation, to proſecute a farther and a more minute inquiry into the principles of the Hindoo religion, I ſhall deem the trivial labour undergone in this reſearch, as moſt amply compenſated.

Without putting etymological proofs to the torture, or moulding to the ſhape of his ſyſtem the generally unſatisfactory and deceitful aids of chronology, the careful obſerver might be enabled to trace ſome points of the religious worſhip of the Hindoo into Egypt.

There he would diſcover the ſacred Bull, or the Cow of Shevah, placed high in the holy legends of the Coptis; he would ſee the Snake, one of the myſterious aſſociates of Sree Mun Narrain, devoutly revered by that nation, as an hieroglyphical emblem of wiſdom and longevity.

It would alſo appear, that the Onion ſo frequently mentioned by hiſtorians and travellers, as held in profound veneration amongſt the Egyptians, is no leſs marked with reverence in Hinduſtan; where, though the uſe of a vegetable diet, is ſo ſtrongly inculcated, and with a few deviations, commonly adopted, the Onion is forbidden to ſome of the ſects of prieſts; and, in the upper part of India, when an oath, on which a matter of conſequence depends, is adminiſtered, the Bramin frequently introduces the Onion to render the ceremony more awful.

On comparing the religious tenets, and the forms of worſhip of the Hindoos, with thoſe of the ancients, there appears in the functions of ſome of the deities, a ſtrong uniformity of likeneſs, which is not unreaſonably placed in the ſame point of view, and were it poſſible to procure a deſcription of the occupations and the various powers of the Hindoo ſubaltern gods, it might be found that the celeſtial group of the weſtern pantheon, had been ſelected from the divine aſſembly of Brimhah.

The Egyptians and the Greeks in their commerce with India, thro' the channel of the Red Sea, have left, I am induced to believe, many tokens behind them of their connection with the Hindoos,

In the collection of a gentleman at Banaris, there are ſeveral valuable antiques, which he purchaſed of the merchants of that city; one of which, repreſenting a Grecian matron, is cut in a ſtyle bearing every mark of a maſterly hand.

There is another, on which Cleopátra is exhibited in the act of being bitten by the aſp.

The ſame gentleman had in his poſſeſſion a Meduſa's head, on an emerald, found alſo at Banaris, which he ſent to England, and it has there been acknowledged to be genuinely Greek.

There was procured at Guzerat, ſome years ago, a very high finiſhed cameo, whereon, Hercules ſlaying the Nemean Lion, was executed in a moſt beautiful and ſtriking manner.

Theſe

Theſe circumſtances are adverted to with ſome ſhew of evincing, that during the intercourſe which exiſted between the natives of Egypt and of India, the former might have introduced into their country, with the rare and luxurious products of Hinduſtan, certain tenets and ceremonies of the Hindoo mythology.

In conſidering of the tract by which theſe antiques were brought into India, I muſt not omit mentioning, that they might have found their way into that country in the cabinets of ſome of the Muſſulman conquerors; who, in the more early period of their empire, were as warm and as enthuſiaſtic admirers of Greek productions and literature as ever the Romans were; and it is a fact, in need of no illuſtration,

illuſtration, that the revival of letters and the arts, after Rome had been ſwallowed up in Gothic ruin, received the moſt potent aid from the Arabian Kaliph, Haroun ul Rachid.

I am ſincerely to lament that my knowledge in aſtronomy is ſo very confined, that I am almoſt wholly incapacitated from deſcribing the attainment which the Bramins had arrived at in that ſcience, long, previouſly to the æra in which it flouriſhed in the weſtern world.

The Zodiac, with its twelve ſigns, is well known to them; and they have beſtowed on the ſeven days, commencing the week with Sunday, the names of the planets.

The

The ſolar year of the Hindoos conſiſts of twelve months, making three hundred and ſixty days, and once in three years they annex an additional month, for the incluſion of thoſe days which are wanting to compleat the exact ſpace of time required by the earth in making its triennial revolution round the ſun.

The days of the month are calculated from the period of the full moon, and the number of them is divided into two equal parts.

To the portion of days comprized in the increaſing half of the moon, they give the name of Sood, or filling; and the other, they term Bole, or the Wain.

The Jogue is divided into luſtra of twelve years, each of which is diſtinguiſhed by its peculiar denomination.

The obſervatory at Banaris is an undeniable proof of the knowledge which the Hindoos have acquired in the motions of the celeſtial bodies.

Could acceſs be gotten to ſuch records of the Hindoos, as are unaccompanied with that redundancy of fable, with which their prieſts have ſo copiouſly interwoven them, it would not be preſumptuous to ſuppoſe, that we ſhould diſcover they were, in the more early age of the world, one of the moſt enlightened and powerful nations then inhabiting the face of the earth.

Their empire, as related in many of their hiſtorical tracts, conſiſted of fifty-ſix ſeparate principalities, ultimately governed by one ruler, whoſe kingdom extended from the ſouthern borders of Tartary to the iſland of Ceylon, and from the confines of Aſſam and Arracan to the river Indus.

This immenſe territory was inhabited by a people divided into four diſtinct tribes, each exerciſing different functions and occupations, and all uniting in their various branches to promote a general good.

It abounded in fair and opulent cities, which were decorated with magnificent and lofty temples for the worſhip of the gods, and with ſumptuous manſions, gardens and fountains

for

for the pleaſure and accommodation of the people.

Uſeful and elegant artiſans, well ſkilled in their various trades, in the raiſing ſtupendous buildings, in the fabricating gold, ſilver, and the moſt delicate cotton cloths, and in the curious workmanſhip of precious ſtones and metals, all found ample encouragement in the exerciſe of their ſeveral profeſſions.

It were almoſt ſuperfluous to ſay, that if ſome glaring indulgences in favor of the ſacred tribe are excepted, Hinduſtan muſt have been governed by ſalutary and well digeſted laws.

From the tranſlation of the code by Mr. Halhed, it is ſeen, that a well choſen ſyſtem of equitable regulations directed the Hindoos in the punishment of crimes, and for the security of property.

The traveller was enabled to journey through this extensive empire with an ease and safety unknown in other countries.

The public roads were shaded with trees; at every halting place a caravansera, with a pond or a well pertaining to it, was founded for the conveniency of the passenger, and should he in any part of the country have been pillaged, and could produce a testimony of his loss, the district in which the damage had been sustained was obliged to make restitution.

When this empire, its polished people, and the progress which art and science

ſcience have made amongſt them, are attentively conſidered and reflected on; when, at the ſame periods, a retroſpective view is thrown on the ſtates of the European world, then immerſed in, or only immerging out of ignorance and barbarity, we muſt behold Hinduſtan with a wonder and reſpect; and we may aſſert, without forfeiting a claim to truth and moderation, that, however far the weſtern nations have, in improvements and refinement, outſtripped the followers of Brimhah, yet in the more early periods of life, they, certainly did poſſeſs valuable materials of philoſophy and uſeful knowledge.

The humane mind, will, naturally, be impreſſed with a ſenſe of ſorrow and pity for a people who have fallen from

from ſo conſpicuous a height of glory and fortune, and who, perhaps, have contributed to poliſh and exalt the very men who now hold them in ſubjection.

To form a ſatisfactory judgment of the genius of the Hindoos, or to deſcribe, with a due accuracy, the degree to which they raiſed art and ſcience, it were requiſite, if the neceſſary materials could be procured, that we did endeavour to exhibit a view of the ſituation in which theſe people were placed before they were conquered by the victorious followers of Mahomed.

A partial and a very degrading relation would be made of them, were the deſcription of their laws, government and manners, taken from the appear-

ance

ance they make in the eye of the world at this day.

The empire of Hinduſtan was overthrown by a fierce race of men, who in their furious courſe of conqueſt, exerted the moſt ſtrenuous efforts, in levelling every monument of worſhip and taſte.

They maſſacred the prieſts and plundered the temples, with a ſpecies of keenneſs and ferocity, which their prophet, himſelf, might have gloried in.

A people thus cruſhed, groaning under the load of oppreſſion, and diſmayed at the ſight of ſuch cruelties, muſt ſoon have loſt the ſpirit of ſcience and the exertion of genius.

Particu-

Particularly, as their fine arts were ſo blended with the ſyſtem of religion, that the perſecution of the one muſt have ſhed the moſt baneful influence on the exiſtence of the other.

To decide on, or affix the character of the Hindoo, from the point of view in which he is now beheld, would be in ſome degree tantamount to an attempt of conveying to the mind an exact idea of antient Greece, from the materials now preſented by that wretched country.

The diſquiſition of the man of philanthropy, and who has ſhaken off the fetters of prejudice, will be far different; he will enjoy an heart-felt pleaſure in contributing his aid towards diſpelling the mortifyng cloud, which

which hath long inveloped the hiſtory of the Hindoo.

This candid inveſtigator will carry him back to that æra of grandeur which his country enjoyed in her day of proſperity, and there hold him out for the inſpection and information of mankind; the generality of whom, whether from motives of contempt or habits of indolence, have acquired but a trivial and a very incorrect knowledge of this antient people.

It will then be ſeen, that the genius of the Hindoos was ſo happily led on, and their bent of diſpoſition ſo aptly regulated and attempered by the rules eſtabliſhed for the performance of their ſeveral occupations and profeſſions, that we are forcibly induced to entertain a moſt reſpectable opinion of the equity of their laws and the wiſdom of their government.

A preciſion, which eradicated the idea of an error, preſcribed to them their reſpective duties in the ſtate and in ſociety, and wholly precluded any one ſect from infringing on the privileges of another.

The Bramin, was inveſted with uncontrolable power in all matters of religion; he became the invariable medium, through which the three inferior claſſes addreſſed their God; he was alſo the ſole repoſitory and diſpenſer of ſcience, and to his care and ability was intruſted the education of youth.

The

The importance of theſe offices muſt have given to the Bramin great ſway in a community, where the attaining at a knowledge of the mode of worſhip from its inexpreſſible variety of ceremony, becomes a taſk of arduous labor, and where at the ſame time it is deemed an obligation indiſpenſably incumbent on the Hindoo for his future welfare, that he be well verſed in the performance of the rites of his religion.

Theſe employments were judged of ſufficient magnitude to occupy the ſtudy and attention of the Bramin, and he was ſtrictly prohibited from engaging in any temporal concern.

The authority of exerciſing every function of royalty ſeems to have devolved, without a reſerve, on the

Chittery or Rajah, and his poſſeſ-ſions were held hereditary in the line of legitimate male primogeniture.

The younger branches of this race had commands in the army beſtowed on them, and they were commonly entruſted with the charge of the forts and the ſtrong holds of the country.

The occupation of a merchant, with the tranſaction of every ſpecies of traffic, was delivered over to the Bhyſe or Baniam, and it was declared unlawful for the other tribes to engage in any branch of commerce.

The huſbandman, the artiſan, the common ſoldier and the labourer, compoſed the ſooder, or the fourth caſt of the Hindoos, and each of theſe respective professions was strongly guarded against encroachments.

Thus distinctly arranged and on the severest penalties, interdicted from any extraneous mixture or the admission of proselytes, the Hindoo government acquired an uniformity and a vigor, the natural result of its happy principles.

Were an analogy ascertained between the mythology of the Hindoos and the Egyptians, very perceptible traces of which present themselves, it may then become a matter of doubt, which people for the greatest space of time have been the most polished and enlightened.

From the adductions which I have brought forward, for the explanation of of ſome of the moſt eſſential tenets of the mythology of the Hindoos, and for the general demonſtration of the antiquity of that nation, it may appear to you, that I maintain the doctrine of Egypt's having received a portion of her ſtock of ſcience and religion from India.

With a deference to popular opinion, but without the prepoſſeſſed determination of fabricating a ſyſtem and adapting to it partial arguments, cautiouſly ſelected for its ſupport, I will confeſs to you, that I am a follower of the belief.

One fact, amongſt ſome others, has afforded me a ſatisfactory proof of the high antiquity of the Hindoos, as a civilized nation, and marks the

ſtrongeſt

ſtrongeſt diſapprobation of any foreign intercourſe.

They are forbidden to croſs the river Attoc, the name of which, in many dialects of their language, ſignifies prohibition, and ſhould they paſs this boundary, they are immediately held unclean, and in the ſtrict ſenſe of their religious law, forfeit their rank in the tribes they may be claſſed in.

It is not, therefore, reaſonable to ſuppoſe that any part of a people, under this reſtriction, and who ſeem to have been ſo centred in themſelves, as to poſitively reject the admiſſion of proſelytes, would have emigrated into a diſtant country, and bring from thence a ſyſtem of religious worſhip.

Let me conclude this comparative review with obſerving, that—When we ſee a people who were poſſeſſed of an ample ſtock of ſcience and well digeſted rules, for the protection and improvement of ſociety, and who profeſſed a religious creed, whoſe tenets conſiſt of the utmoſt refinement and variety of ceremony, and at the ſame time, obſerve, amongſt other Aſiatic nations, and the Egyptians of former times, but partial diſtributions of this knowledge, law and religion, we are led to entertain a ſuppoſition—that the proprietors of the leſſer have been ſupplied from the ſources of the greater fund.

If the poſitions which I have ſtated, are thought to convey reaſon, they will afford greater pleaſure to the man of

curious

curious ſtudy than thoſe unſubſtantial and confuſed chronological proofs, which are often framed as they may moſt commodiouſly accord with ſome favorite Hypotheſis.

Amongſt the Hindoos, marriage*, when it can be performed with any degree of conveniency, is deemed a religious duty of an indiſpenſable nature; and it is believed, that propagating ſpecies in that ſtate, entitles parents to ſingular marks of divine favor.

* This word, in the Sumſcrit language, ſignifies pleaſure. The Hindoos in common uſage have but one wife, and when this rule is deviated from, it is conſidered as an indecency. There is a ſet of mendicants, called Joquees or Byraghees, who live in a ſtate of celibacy, but it is not a numerous one.

They ſhew a diſapprobation of celibacy by many marks of opprobrium and ſcorn ; and, I have frequently obſerved, that when a Hindoo has been aſked if he was a married man, he has appeared diſconcerted, and aſhamed at the fact obliging him to anſwer in the negative, and immediately attributed the cauſe of his ſituation to ſome particular misfortune.

It is to this inſtitution, which is ſo ſtrongly recommended, and from a ſtigma being affixed on the non-obedience to it, I may ſay, even enforced—that the generally great population of Hinduſtan, and its ſpeedy recovery after the calamities of war and famine, muſt be largely aſcribed.

The

The entire ſyſtem of the domeſtic ordinances and œconomy of the Hindoos, is founded on a ſtrong, yet a ſimple baſis, out of which ariſe effects the moſt happy in themſelves, and powerfully operative in uniting the leading bonds of ſociety.

From the eſtabliſhed laws and uſage of the country, the wife depends for the enjoyment of every pleaſure, as well as for the mere ordinary accommodations of life, on the immediate exiſtence of her huſband.

It becomes her invariable intereſt to preſerve his health, and her happineſs is abſolutely centred on his living to an old age.

On the demiſe of the huſband, his wife, literally, devolves into a *caput mortuum*, ſhe cannot marry again, ſhe is deprived of all conſequence in the family, and is diveſted of every mark of ornament and diſtinction.

There are certain religious ceremonies not lawful for her to perform; and, in ſome inſtances, ſhe is held unclean; but, on all occaſions, after her huſband's death, the widow is claſſed in the houſe as a ſlave, or a menial ſervant.

Amongſt the three firſt caſts of Hindoos, where the idea of honour is more refined, and is oftentimes carried to an extreme, rather than ſuffer this gradation, by which every female attraction is extinguiſhed, and the women themſelves reduced to the loweſt degree of mortification, on the pretence

pretence of matrimonial affection, they frequently devote themselves on the funeral pile of their husbands.

In addition to the dread of so degraded a state of humiliation, the widow, on the other side, is told by the Bramins, that in consequence of performing this act of heroism, she will partake of the most exquisite future joys, and that her progeny will become the immediate charge of the deity.

Though the issue of such a resolution must forcibly affect the feelings of humanity, yet as it would appear to originate in a principle, tending to strengthen a salutary domestic policy, it ought not to be hastily condemned as a custom wholly cruel and unjust.

Conformably to the ſtate of domeſtic ſubordination, in which Hindoo women are placed, it has been judged expedient to debar them from the uſe of letters.

The Hindoos invariably hold the language, that female acquired accompliſhments are not neceſſary; whether for the purpoſe of contributing to a woman's own happineſs, or for preſerving that decorum of character, and ſimplicity of manners, which alone can render her uſeful or amiable in the eſtimation of her family.

They urge, that a knowledge of literature would have an injurious tendency in drawing a woman from her houſehold cares, and would conduce to give her a diſreliſh to thoſe offices

in

in which are centered the only ſatiſfaction and amuſement that ſhe can with propriety and an obſervance of rectitude, partake of; and ſuch is the force of cuſtom, that a Hindoo woman would incur a ſevere reproach were it known, that ſhe could read or write.

The dancing girls, whoſe occupations are avowedly devoted to the pleaſures of the public, are on the contrary educated in moſt branches of learning, with the utmoſt care, and are minutely inſtructed in the knowledge of every attraction and blandiſhment which can operate in communicating the moſt refined pleaſures.

You

You will be pleaſed to obſerve, that theſe women are not obliged to ſhelter themſelves in private haunts, or are they, on account of their profeſſional conduct, marked with any opprobious ſtigma.

They compoſe a particular claſs of the ſociety they may have been originally attached to, and enjoy the declared protection and ſanction of government, for which they are aſſeſſed according to their ſeveral capacities.

No religious ceremonies or feſtival of any kind is thought to be performed with the order requiſite, unleſs acpanied with dancing girls, and it is uſual for them on a fixed day in the week to attend at the court of the prince or governor of the diſtrict, either

either to make their obeiſance, or exhibit ſome entertainment.

And as a compenſation for ſuch ſervices, they are endowed with certain grants of government lands.

An Hindoo family, is implicitly governed by the male ſenior in it, to whom there is ſhewn every token of reverence and reſpect.

A ſon will not ſit in the preſence of his father without an expreſs deſire, and in his deportment and converſation obſerves to him the moſt affectionate behaviour.

In the courſe of my reſidence in India, and acquaintance with the Hindoos, I have known but few inſtances of female incontinence amongſt their married women, and not one of direct undutifulneſs to parents.

I cannot avoid obſerving, alſo, in this place, that I never heard of a Hindoo free-thinker, and that their moſt illuſtrious characters, and men of the world, ſuch as Scindia, Nanah Purnawees* &c. believe the tenets of their doctrine with as much ſincerity, and practiſe the moſt minute ceremony with as much ſcrupulous attention as the ſimpleſt peaſant in their country.

* Eminent Mhahrattah chiefs.

Extract

Extract of a Letter written at Kachmire, April, 1783.

THE religion which prevails in these parts*, is that of Brimhah, and as I have already in a ſmall ſketch endeavoured to throw ſome light on that ancient and curious ſyſtem of worſhip, I will now paſs it over, with an offer of preſenting thoſe remarks to you ſhould you ever be diſpoſed to read them.

There does not exiſt a greater difference in the manners of the inhabitants of theſe mountains, and the people of your quarter, than generally does between high and low landers of the ſame nation.

 I took

* The mountains at the head of the Punjab.

I took notice of two ufages, which feem peculiar to thefe mountaineers, that of not fhaving the beard, and embracing; this ceremony is performed by inclining the head over the left fhoulder of the party embraced, and is never ufed more than one time at a meeting.

The cuftom of permitting the beard to grow, proceeds, perhaps, from a certain ferocity and roughnefs immediately incident to their fituation, and predominant in the difpofition of all mountaineers; which, prompts them in different modes to fhew their difdain and contempt of the fofter and more luxurious manners of their low country neighbours,

The

The embracing over the left ſhoulders only, take its riſe, I would conjecture, from the deſire of having the right hand at liberty in caſe of danger.

The women have bright olive complexions, are pretty, and moſt delicately ſhaped.

There is a pleaſing freedom in their manners, which without having any tendency to immodeſty, or ſeeming to ariſe from habits of licentiouſneſs, ſtrikes you, as the ſimple reſult of that unlimited confidence which the Hindoo huſbands in general repoſe in their wives.

I have known the women to ſtop in the way, though a pot of water has been on their heads, and converſe unreſervedly

ſervedly with paſſengers, directing them with great good nature and civility in the right road, or communicating to them any other common information.

Their dreſs I think, is agreeable and decent, conſiſting of a petticoat with a border, commonly of a different colour, and a cloſe jacket, which comes half way down the waiſt, and, from the bottom of the fore part of it, drops a looſe ſtomacher, which reaches to the girdle.

Their hair, which is held by them in as high an eſtimation as that beautiful ornament can be regarded by our gayeſt weſtern females, is plaited and interwoven with black ſilk or cotton

ſtrings,

ſtrings, which falling down the back, almoſt ſweeps the ground.

Over this dreſs, they throw in a moſt becoming and graceful faſhion, a veil, which ſeldom touches, but never wholly conceals the face.

The women of the principal people are kept in Zinanahs, as amongſt the Muſſulmen, and this practice exiſting in a country*, were little danger is to be apprehended from the inſpection of foreign viſitants, affords ſome reaſon of believing, that the concealing certain ranks of women has been a cuſtom eſtabliſhed amongſt the Hindoos, previouſly to the date of any Mahometan government, in Hinduſtan.

It

* Mountainous and difficult of acceſs.

It was once my opinion that the Hindoos, adopting the ufage of their Muffulman conquerors—who deem females in the iffue of war a lawful prize, had fecluded them from public view.

But feeing thefe mountaineers practifing the fame mode, and knowing alfo that the Mhahrattahs, who are an independent people, and confequently free from the apprehenfions, which the conquered Hindoos may entertain, ufe Zinanahs for their women of rank; I am induced to think, that this cuftom did prevail in India before the æra of the Mahometan invafion.

At the fame time, were I to hazard an opinion on fome of the manners of the

the Hindoos from their hiſtory; the beſt of which, I am to obſerve, is ravelled in a maze of obſcurity and fable, I would ſay, that the Hindoos in former times, did not confine any claſſes of their women.

But as their manners from the great influx of wealth and luxury amongſt them became leſs ſimple, though they are a people who have undergone fewer changes than any other, that the Princes of the country produced this innovation for the purpoſe of impreſſing in the minds of their ſubjects, an awe and reſpect for their families.

In the different relations of the incarnations of Vyſtnou, and in the hiſtory of their antient Princes, it is ſeen, that at thoſe periods, the Hindoo women had an unreſtrained admiſſion into the aſſemblies of men, and oftentimes poſſeſſed great ſway in them.

In the hiſtory of Ram, who, you know, my dear ſir, made a great figure on earth, I have met with a paſſage, which may ſerve to illuſtrate this poſition, and trace alſo to a high ſource, a mode of trial hitherto practiſed in Europe.

I will premiſe, with informing you, that Sree Mun Narrain, the Grand Deity of the Hindoos, together with his indiviſible aſſociates, the Mhah Letchimy and the Snake, with the view of correcting certain evils and abuſes which at that time had deranged

ranged the terreſtrial ſyſtem, found it expedient to perſonify human beings.

Narrain, acccordingly, took on him the form of Ram, a renowned ſoldier, Letchimy became his wife, under the name of Seetah Devee, and the Snake was transformed into the body of a Letchimun, the brother and conſtant attendant of Ram.

Under this deſignation, theſe perſonages mixed freely in all human ſocieties, nor is there the leaſt mention made in any part of the hiſtory of Seetah's having been reſtricted from an admiſſion to them.

On the contrary, ſhe is repreſented as bearing a part on every occaſion,

 where

where it might have been proper for her ſex to appear.

A ſervice of a dangerous nature required, that Ram ſhould leave Seetah behind him, and the party being then in a deſart, ſhe was conſigned to the charge of Letchimun, until Ram might return.

Seetah and her companion remained ſome time in perfect ſecurity and quiet, when a famed magician, led on doubtleſs by the devil, who is ever on the watch to draw aſtray the ladies, came that way, ſaw Seetah, and became deeply enamoured with her.

This ſubtle man having diſcovered, perhaps, by his ſpells and incantations, that the eyes of women are the ſooneſt enſnared, contrived that a bird

of

of a moſt brilliantly beautiful plumage, ſhould fly full in the ſight of Seetah.

This horrid experiment had the deſired and the completeſt effect ; for the deluded fair one inſtantly conjured Letchimun, by every thing he could hold dear, by the affection he had for her, by the reſpect he bore to Ram, to procure for her the charming bird.

Letchimun was amazed and much troubled at this entreaty : he endeavored to expoſtulate on the eminent danger of quitting her in ſo perilous a ſituation.

He pointed out to her, in the moſt lively language, the certainty of incurring the ſevereſt diſpleaſure of Ram, for a breach of his orders ; and, in

ſhort,

ſhort, he urged every argument which a regard for his own character, or her ſafety, could ſuggeſt.

The dazzling hues of this bird had taken ſuch ample poſſeſſion of the mind of Seetah, that there did not remain in it one unoccupied ſpace for the reception of Letchimun's advice.

She muſt poſſeſs this object of her wiſhes, or ſhe ſhould become the moſt miſerable of women; and, on the repeated denial of Letchimun to comply with her deſire, blinded by the diſappointment of her fondeſt hopes, and hurried on by a burſt of rage, ſhe accuſed Letchimun of the deſign of ſeducing her, and alledged that as the only reaſon of his diſlike of leaving her.

This accuſation convincing Letchimun of the inefficacy of his arguments, and the neceſſity of an acquieſcence, he immediately went in queſt of the bird; but, previouſly to his departure, he drew a magic circle around the ſpot where Seetah remained; and told her, while ſhe continued within that ſpace, that no misfortune could betide her.

Letchimun had no ſooner gone, than the plotting necromancer, aſſuming the appearance of an old and a very infirm man, in a languid and a feeble manner approached near the place where Seetah ſtood, and through exceſs of weakneſs, he ſeemed obliged to extend himſelf on the ground.

He beſought her, in an affecting and a pitiable tone of voice, to adminiſter

to

to him a little water to allay his thirſt, and to recruit an almoſt exhauſted ſtrength.

The tender hearted, but ill-fated Seetah felt the full force of the prayers of a diſtreſſed old man, and with a boſom overflowing with the effuſions of humanity and benevolence, unmindful of her own happineſs, ſhe ſtepped beyond the preſcribed bound, and fell that inſtant into the power of her betrayer.

Here the ſtory ſets forth, what would but little contribute to my credit to relate, or your amuſement to be informed of; it only now concerns me to make mention, that after Ram had recovered Seetah, he ordered, for the removal of every ſuſpicion in his own breaſt,

breaſt, and for effectually ſhutting the mouth of Slander, that ſhe ſhould undergo the ordeal trial.

Seetah, eager to baniſh the moſt latent doubt from the mind of her Lord, and anxious to exhibit to the world ſo public a teſtimony of her purity, heard the mandate with pleaſure; and, without any ſhew of dread, walked over the burning iron; but the feet of Seetah, ſays the hiſtorian, being ſhod with innocence, the ſcorching heat was to her as a bed of flowers.

Pardon me, my friend, for thus intruding on you this eaſtern tale, which would be altogether a trifling one, did it not tend to indicate, that the

Hindoos had a knowledge of the ordeal trial, at, doubtleſs, a very early period, and that in thoſe ages it would ſeem their women of the firſt rank appeared in public.

The ſame uſe may be made of this ſtory, as that which is contained in the Arabian Nights entertainment, where amidſt the olio of taliſmans, genii and devils, you are enabled to extract juſt repreſentations of the manners and diſpoſitions of the people.

As I have thus far entered into a ſubject, which has often excited my curioſity, I will, with your permiſſion, proceed ſomewhat farther, and recite to you a circumſtance which may aſſiſt in corroborating my belief, that the Hindoo women of rank, conformably

to

to ancient uſages, and to ſome now exiſting, were not wholly ſecluded from the ſight of men.

When a young woman of the Rajah or the Royal Race, was marriageable, or ſuppoſed to poſſeſs an underſtanding diſcrimination of choice, ſhe was conducted into an apartment, where there were many youths of her own ſex aſſembled, and deſired to ſelect the perſon the moſt pleaſing to her.

She performed the ceremony, of declaring her ſentiments, by throwing a wreath of flowers over the neck of the favored young man, who, if the lady ſhould have been agreeable to him, was eſteemed her future huſband.

This rule, I have been informed, is obſerved at this day in Tanjore, where I reſided ſome little time, and received the intelligence from a Mharattah Bramin, who had an employment at the Rajah's court.

The aforegoing opinions, my friend, I have freely given you, and I am to intreat, that you will as freely diſſect and analyſe them; taking ſuch parts as may appear to you founded on reaſon and natural principles, and rejecting ſuch as may ſeem vague or dictated by fancy.

F I N I S.